The Absolute Beginner's Guide To Coding Using Scratch

By: Nicole Yarroch & Leo C. Ureel II

Table Of Contents

Why Learn To Code?

All About Scratch

Have you ever wondered how websites are built, how video games are created, or how apps for smartphones are designed?

They were all made with a programming language, which is a special language that allows people to communicate with computers.

What is Scratch?
One of the many programming languages available is Scratch. People like to program with Scratch because it is easy to get started. Scratch is a visual programming language, which means you will be able to quickly figure out how to make the computer perform complex tasks.

When you write a program in Scratch, you are making a list of instructions for the computer to follow. A computer's job is to follow instructions. In fact, a computer follows millions of instructions every second.

Your job is to learn how to communicate with the computer so it will follow your instructions. Don't worry, learning how to code is not hard at all, and you will soon be well on your way to creating your own computer programs.

Getting Scratch

Scratch is a free programming language that runs over the internet. You can program in Scratch from your home computer by visiting the Scratch website at:

https://scratch.mit.edu

Scratch requires Adobe Flash to run on Macs, Windows, and Linux. You can get Flash at:

https://get.adobe.com/flashplayer

If Scratch does not work on your computer, you can use a very similar language called Snap!, which also runs over the internet but does not require Flash.

http://snap.berkeley.edu

Snap! is almost identical to Scratch and most of the programs you write in this book will work in either language.

Create Your First Program

Go to the Scratch website and click the **Create** menu item at the top of the web page. When you first open Scratch you will see something similar to the sketch below.

Stage | Block Palette | Script Area

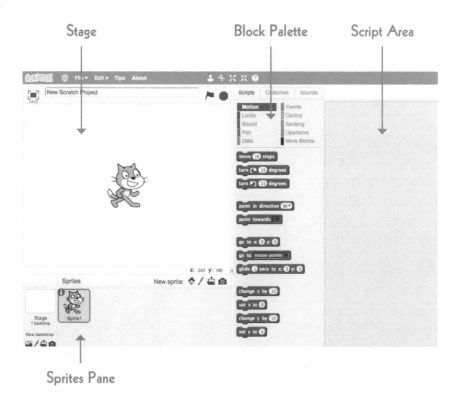

Sprites Pane

One of the first thing you will notice is that there is a picture of a cat in the middle of the stage area. The cat is called a sprite. A sprite is an object that performs actions in the program. You can change your sprite's image by clicking on the **Costumes Tab** in the **Block Palette**.

Making a program in Scratch is a snap because everything we want to tell the computer to do can be made by fitting together the command blocks. For our first program we will make the cat say "Hello World."

Step 1) The first thing we need is a way to start the program running. Click on **Events** in the block palette.

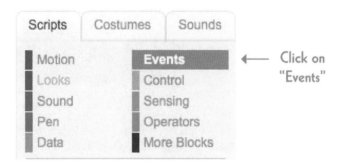

Step 2) This will reveal the event command blocks. We would like the program to start running whenever the green flag above the stage area is clicked. Drag the when flag clicked block into the script area.

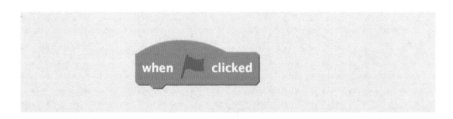

Step 3) Next, click on **Looks** in the block palette. Drag the say block into the script area, connecting it to the

when flag clicked block.

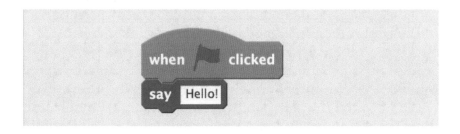

Step 4) Double click the word "Hello!" and replace it by typing in "Hello World".

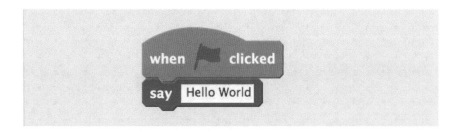

Step 5) Run your program You have written your first program in Scratch! To run your program, click on the green flag above the stage area. You should see your sprite say "Hello World."

Draw a Square

Drawing in Scratch is a lot like drawing with a pen and paper, except in order to draw something in Scratch, you have to tell the computer in which direction to draw the line and how far to draw the line.

For the examples in this book we will use a *sprite* that looks like a green triangle when drawing. You can think of this triangle as a pen. Whichever direction the pen is pointing is the direction the line will be drawn. You can change the sprite costume to any design you want.

Step 1) The first thing you need to do is draw a straight line. To do this, you will need to put the pen down. Pen down is a command block in the *Pen* section of the block palette. Then you will need to move the sprite. Move is a command in the *Motion* section. Set move to 50 steps.

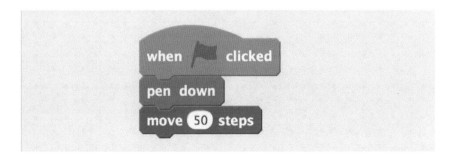

Step 2) When you click on the green flag, the pen will move across the screen, and there will be a line from where the pen started to where the pen ended.

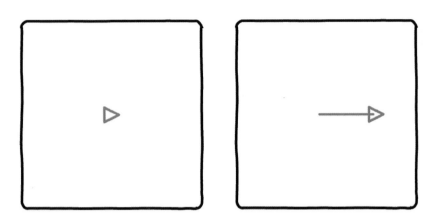

Step 3) Now you want to draw the next side of the square. To change the direction of the pen use the turn clockwise block. Set the turn to 90 degrees.

This tells the program to rotate the pen 90 degrees to the right. The pen will change direction and will now be facing down.

Draw the second side of the square by connecting another move 50 steps block. Your code should look like this:

```
when [flag] clicked
pen down
move 50 steps
turn ↻ 90 degrees
move 50 steps
```

When your program runs (click the green flag), it should draw two sides of a square like so:

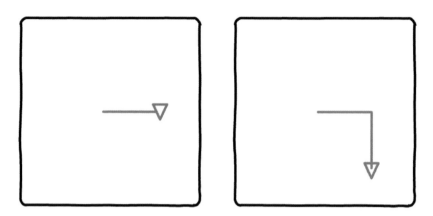

Step 4) Can see where this is going? Snap together a couple more turn and move command blocks to complete your square.

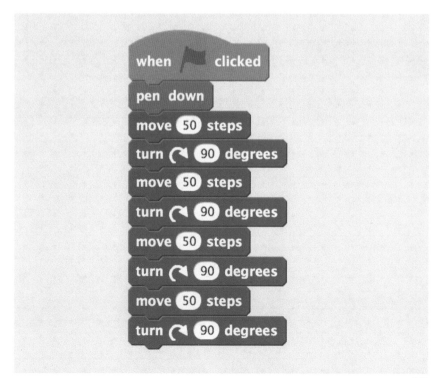

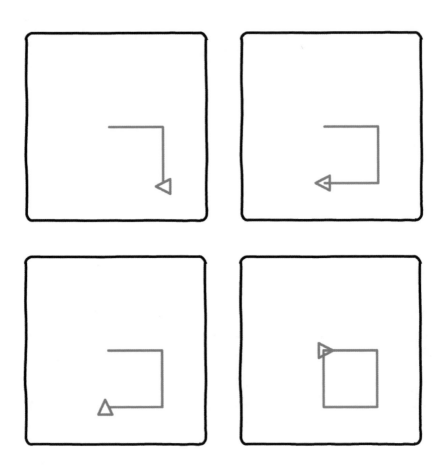

You have created a square using command blocks! In future chapters we will learn how to draw triangles and circles.

Ch 3: Practice Problems

1) Can you draw a house by adding a triangle on top of the rectangle you drew in this chapter?

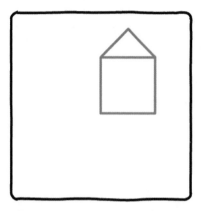

2) Try drawing a square that has been rotated 45 degrees. It is very similar to the square that you drew in this chapter except the intial angle of the pen is 45 degrees instead of 90 degrees.

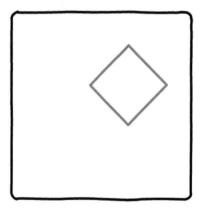

Delete Your Drawing

Clear The Stage After you have experimented with drawing, you may want to clear your stage so you can start anew. The fastest way to clear the stage is to use the clear command from the *Pen* section of the block palette. Drag the clear command to the script area and double click on the button.

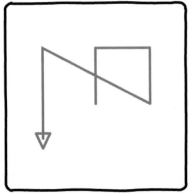
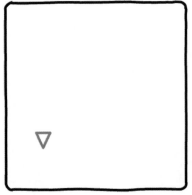

Return Home If you want to return your triangle to the middle of the screen, you can use the commands:

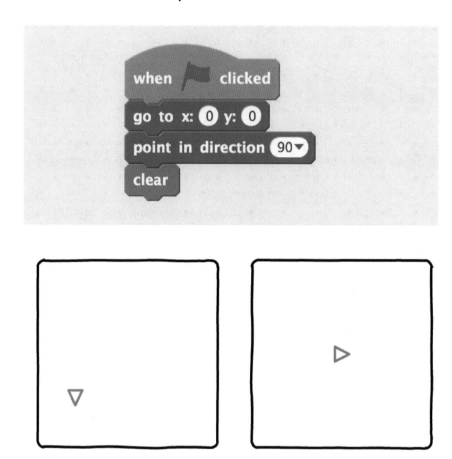

Repeat Command

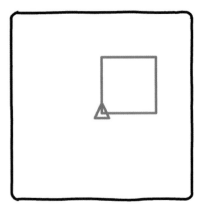

You may have noticed that in the last program you used the two commands, move and turn clockwise, four times each. There is a way to shorten this task so you only have to type each command once. Do this by using the repeat command found in the block palette.

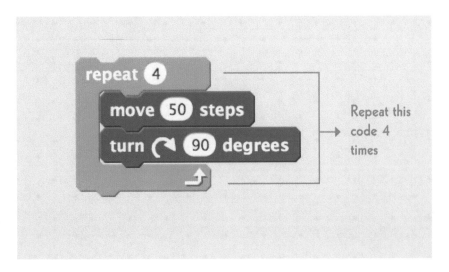

Repeat this code 4 times

Square with Repeat

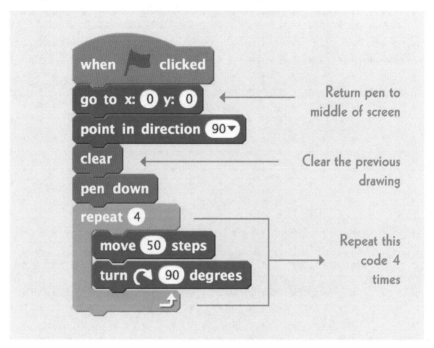

when 🚩 clicked
go to x: 0 y: 0 ← Return pen to middle of screen
point in direction 90▾
clear ← Clear the previous drawing
pen down
repeat 4
    move 50 steps
    turn ↻ 90 degrees ⟶ Repeat this code 4 times

Drawing a Circle

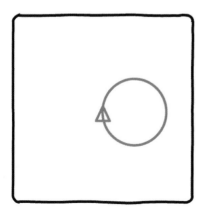

Drawing a circle on a computer is different from drawing a circle by hand. A computer can only draw straight lines, but you can create the appearance of a curved line by drawing a bunch of tiny lines that, when connected together, look like a circle.

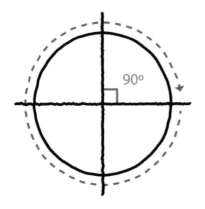

Since a circle has 360 degrees, you can create a circle by making 360 tiny lines, each one step long. After each line is drawn, you turn the pen 1 degree to the right and move another step. Together, all the tiny little steps will look like a circle!

```
when [flag] clicked
go to x: 0 y: 0
point in direction 90▼
clear
pen down
repeat 360
    move 1 steps
    turn ↻ 1 degrees
```

Drawing Two Circles

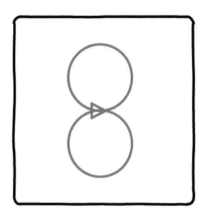

What if you wanted to draw a circle to the left? You could repeat the same commands except change the command from turn clockwise to the opposite command turn counter-clockwise.

when 🏳 clicked

go to x: 0 y: 0

point in direction 90▾

clear

pen down

repeat 360
  move 1 steps
  turn ↻ 1 degrees

repeat 360
  move 1 steps
  turn ↺ 1 degrees

Drawing a Triangle

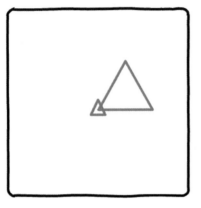

You can also use the repeat command to easily make an equilateral triangle (a triangle in which the lengths of all three sides are equal). Since each of the internal angles must also be equal we can create a triangle by rotating the pen 120 degrees after each line is drawn.

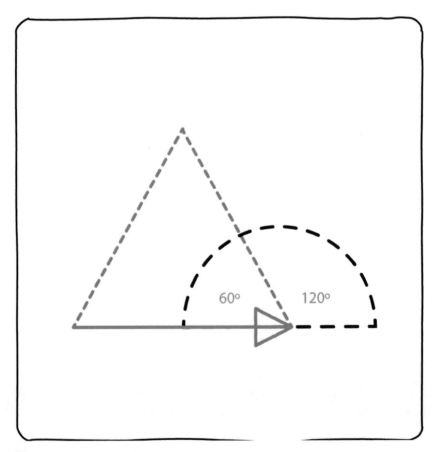

Why do you need to rotate 120 degrees and not 60 degrees? This is because you need to take into account the direction the pen is facing. In order to position the pen so the next line will be 60 degrees from the last line, you need to rotate the pen 120 degrees counter-clockwise.

Calculating Angles To quickly figure out how many degrees to rotate the pen when creating an equilateral shape, simply divide 360 degrees by the number of sides in your shape. For example, if you have five sides, you will need to rotate 72 degrees between each line because 360/5 is equal to 72. Six sides is 60 degrees, and eight sides is 45 degrees.

Ch 5: Practice Problems

1) Can you draw a small circle nested inside a big circle?

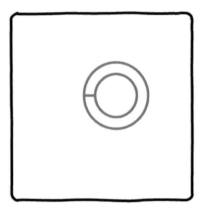

2) Try drawing a hexagon (a shape with 6 sides). To figure out the angles between the lines, divide 360 degrees by the number of sides.

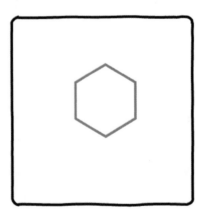

Nested Repeats

06

The really cool thing about repeat is that it allows you to draw the same shape as many times as you want with only a few lines of code.

In the last chapter you learned about using the repeat command. You can also nest a repeat command inside another repeat command. This permits the building of more complex shapes.

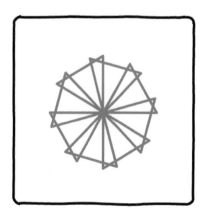

Nested loops can look a little complicated the first time you see them, so lets go through the code line by line for the drawing on the left.

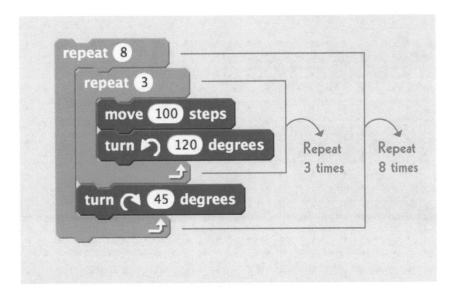

Step 1) First, Scratch does the inner repeat command repeat 3[move 100 steps, turn right 120 degrees]. This creates a triangle.

Step 2) Scratch then does the turn right 45 degrees. This turns the pen right by 45 degrees.

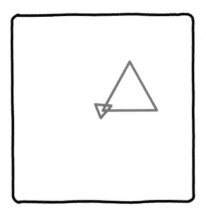

Step 3) After these two steps, the sprite has drawn a triangle. Rotating by 45 degrees prevents the sprite from drawing right over the first triangle.

Step 4) The sprite then does steps 1 and 2 again. The screen now looks like this:

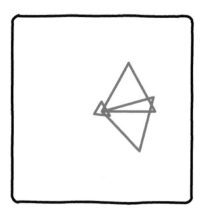

Step 5) The sprite continues to do steps 1 and 2 until it has repeated the steps 8 times. After the 8th time, Scratch stops. The final screen looks like this:

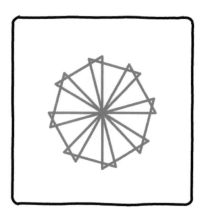

Nested Repeats with Different Shapes

You can make lots of interesting shapes by repeating a simple shape over and over again. Other shapes that you could use as a base are circles, pentagons (shapes with 5 sides), and octagons (shapes with 8 sides).

```
repeat 8
    repeat 36
        move 10 steps
        turn ↻ 10 degrees
    turn ↻ 45 degrees
```

What would happen if you repeated the outer loop 36 times? Or if you changed the angle the pen rotates from 45 degrees to 10 degrees?

Ch 6: Practice Problems

1) Try to draw the shape below. It is just a repeat of a hexagon shape (a shape with 6 sides).

2) Revise the nested code for the circle shape in this chapter to add more circles to the shape.

Making Colors

07

So far you have only been able to draw with the color black, but you can change the color of the pen to any color that you want.

You can think of pen colors as a rainbow that ranges from red to yellow to green to blue and back to red.

0 ▭▭▭▭▭▭▭▭▭▭▭▭▭▭▭▭▭▭▭▭ **200**

You can find the set pen color to block in the *Pen* section of the block palette. The block takes a number between 0 and 199. A value of 200 is the same color as a 0 value. This means that whenever you change the pen color by adding 200 to the current pen value, the color looks the same.

> set pen color to **0**

The easiest way to create a color is to use the color picker version of the set pen color to block. Set the color by clicking on the current color square in the block, and then click on any color anywhere on your computer screen to use that color.

How To Use the Color Codes In the code example below, the color is set to red before the rectangle is drawn. Notice that the values in change pen color to are the same as the color values in the table on the next page.

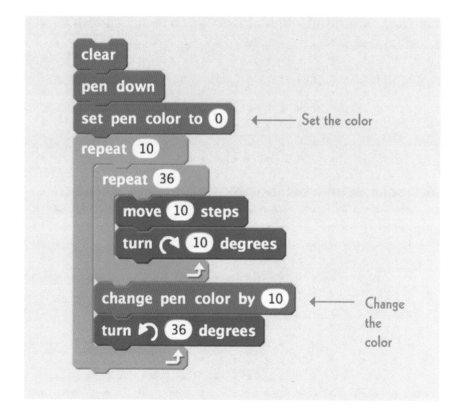

Common Colors			
Color	RGB Value	Color	RGB Value
Red	0	Yellow	33
Green	66	Cyan	99
Blue	132	Magenta	165

Random Colors To create random colors, you need to generate random values. There is an Operator Block called pick random that allows you to pick a random number between two values.

The example above tells Scratch to pick a number between 1 and 200. In the next project you will learn how to generate random colors while drawing.

Project: Nested Circles with Random Colors

In this code example, the color was changed inside the repeat 15 block. This ensures that each separate circle is drawn with a different color. Try seeing what will happen if you move the change pen color block to inside the repeat 36 block.

```
when [flag] clicked
go to x: 0 y: 0
point in direction 90▼
clear
pen down
repeat 15
    repeat 36
        move 10 steps
        turn ↺ 10 degrees
    turn ↻ 24 degrees
    change pen color by (pick random 10 to 30)
```

All About Variables

08

What is a Variable? Sometimes you want to be able to keep track of a value that might change as the code executes. In order to keep track of that value, you need to store it in memory so it can be accessed again. Variables are a way for programmers to store values. It is helpful to think of a variable as a box that can only store one value. When a new value is put in the box, the old value is destroyed forever.

How to Create a Variable Go to the Data Section in the *Block Palette* and click the "*Make A Variable*" button. Then enter the name for the variable and click

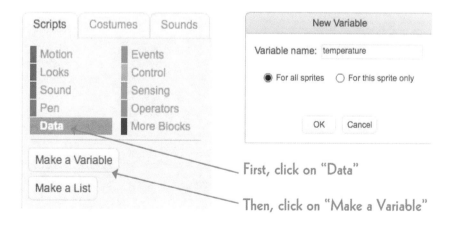

First, click on "Data"

Then, click on "Make a Variable"

"*OK.*" You can give the variable any name that you want. When you use the variable name in your program, you will be able to get the value stored in memory.

After you click "*OK,*" you will then see some new command blocks in the Data Section that can be used to set the value of your variable.

Make a Variable

☑ angle

☑ temperature

set angle to 0

change angle by 1

show variable angle

hide variable angle

Make a List

Changing the Value of a Variable At some point you will want to change the value stored in a variable. You can set the value to a specific number or you can perform some math on the variable already being stored. Math can be done using the blocks in the Operator Section.

Math Commands		
Command	**Math**	**Command In Scratch**
add	2 + 4	2 + 4
subtract	5 - 9	5 - 9
multiply	2 * 2	2 * 2
divide	8 / 4	8 / 4

Project: Make a Spiral

When drawing a spiral, you need to adjust the angle of pen after each line segment is drawn. Now that you have learned about variables, it will be easy to draw a spiral because you can store the angle value in a variable.

How Variables Work When you first start the program, the value stored in the variable named "angle" is 0. As the program progresses, you may want to change the value stored "angle." To do this, you can use the set block to change the value of the variable.

Getting the Value of a Variable After you make a new variable, there is a new oval block with the variable name in the Data Block section. This variable block can be dragged onto any other block that has a placeholder.

When you draw a spiral, you need to adjust the angle of the pen after each line segment is drawn. Now that you have learned about variables, it will be easy for you to draw a spiral because you can store the angle value in a variable.

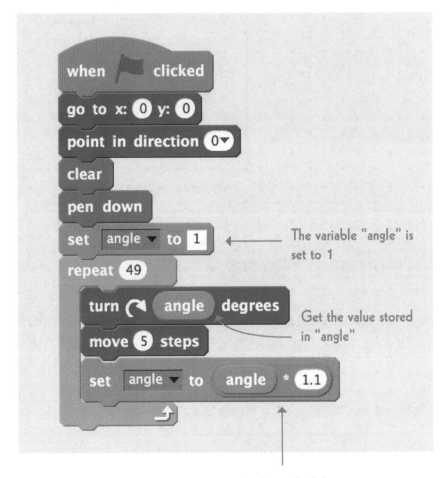

when ⚑ clicked

go to x: 0 y: 0

point in direction 0▾

clear

pen down

set angle ▾ to 1 ⟵——— The variable "angle" is set to 1

repeat 49

    turn ↻ angle degrees — Get the value stored in "angle"

    move 5 steps

    set angle ▾ to angle * 1.1

At the end of the repeat loop, increase the value stored in "angle" by multiplying it by 1.1

Ch 8: Practice Problems

1) True or False. Are these two variable names the same: "myFirstVariable" and "MYFIRSTVARIABLE"?

2) What is the final value stored in w after the program executes?

The final value of w is: _____

3) What is the final value stored in w after the program executes?

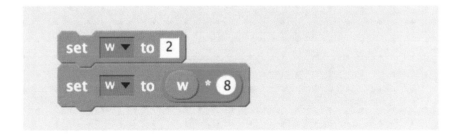

The final value of w is: _____

Awesome Functions

09

Why Use Functions? When you used the repeat command, it made drawing complex shapes really easy. Now you will learn about functions, which allow you to repeat the same code over and over again without having to rewrite the code. A function may sound an awful lot like the repeat command, but functions are one of the most useful tools a programmer can have because it allows you to adjust certain parts of the code based on your needs.

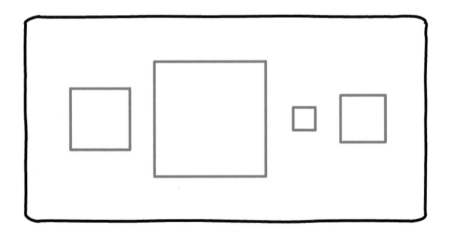

The limitation of the repeat command is apparent when you want to draw a bunch of differnt size squares. Each square will be coded with virtually identical code except for the length of the sides. With a function, we can use one block of code to draw different size squares!

Formatting Functions Functions have to be written in a particular way. A function must have a name and it may have zero or it may have multiple inputs.

Inputs Scratch offers three different types of inputs: number, string, and boolean. Strings are words like "hello" or "program." Booleans can have only two values: true or false. Finally, numbers are values like 23.56 or 200.

Create a Function To create a function, go to the More Blocks section and click on the *"Make a Block"* button. Then, enter a name for your function. If your function needs to use input values, click on one of the options and enter a name for the input.

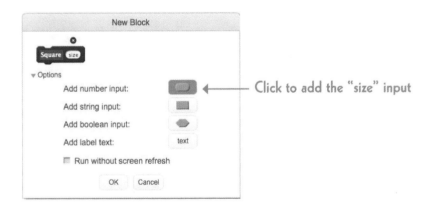

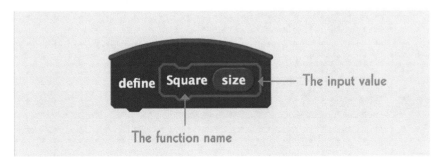

Calling A Function You can make a script attached to a define block and click "run," but nothing will happen. This is because you have to tell the computer to call the function. The way you call the "Square" function defined on the previous page is by using the following command block, which was created at the same time as the function.

In the example above, the input value is 50, but it could be set to any number.

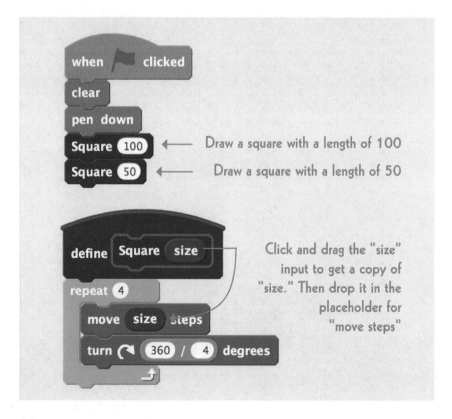

Project: Drawing Squares

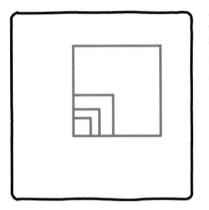

Let's use a function to draw a bunch of different size squares. Can you draw some other size squares?

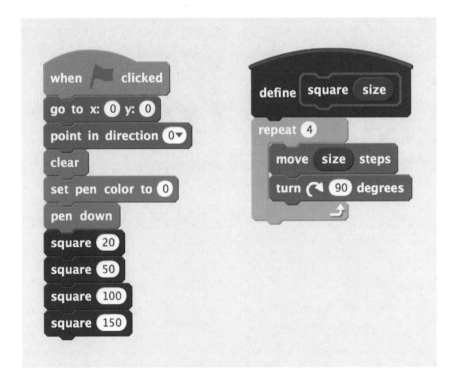

Project: Spiral Rose

You can combine repeats and functions to make the spiral rose to the left.

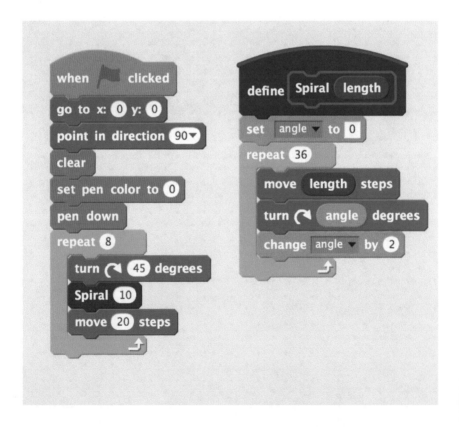

Project: Circle of Squares

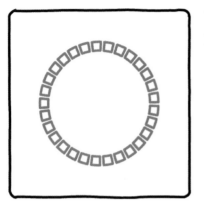

You can make a lot of complicated things easily with functions. In this function, the command penup is used to stop the pen from making marks while it is moving.

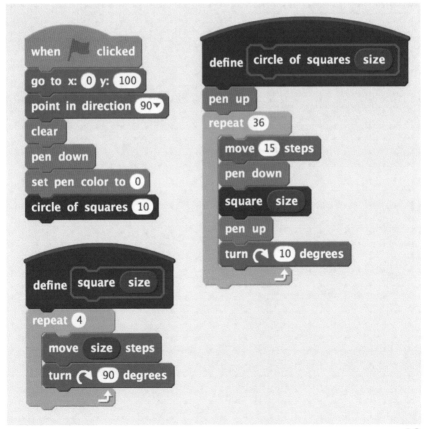

Ch 9: Practice Problems

1) Can you make a function that will help you draw different size triangles?

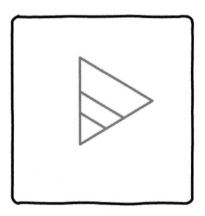

2) Make a function that will let you draw different size houses.

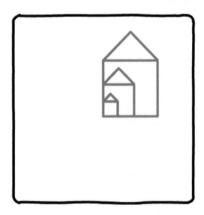

If
Statements

10

What if you wanted your pen to do different things based on the current value of a variable? If the variable's value is greater than zero, the pen should rotate 45 degrees. If the variable's value is equal to zero, the pen should rotate 90 degrees. An easy way to program this is to use an if statement.

If Statement The if statement tells your program to execute a certain section of code only if a particular condition is true. If it is true, the code between the brackets will be executed. If it is false, Scratch will simply ignore the code between the brackets.

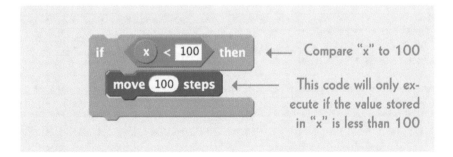

←—— Compare "x" to 100

←—— This code will only execute if the value stored in "x" is less than 100

Conditional Statements Scratch lets you compare values to see if one is greater than the other, less than the other, or equal to the other value.

Conditional Statements

Command	Example	Command In Scratch
equal to	5 = 6	`5 = 6`
less than	10 < 3	`10 < 3`
greater than	8 > 5	`8 > 5`

Project: Radiating Lines

To make the image to the left, use two if statements to adjust the length of the lines.

The repeat command is going to run 73 times. You are going to use a variable called count to keep track of what number repeat we are on. If the count is less than 36, decrease the line length. If the count is greater than 36, increase the line length.

You can use this technique to draw different shapes depending on your if statements. What will happen if you use four if statements instead of the two in the example?

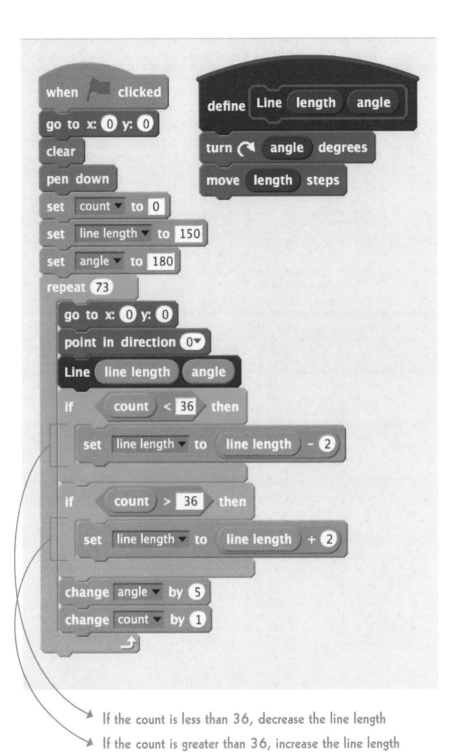

when 🏁 clicked
go to x: 0 y: 0
clear
pen down
set count to 0
set line length to 150
set angle to 180
repeat 73
  go to x: 0 y: 0
  point in direction 0▾
  Line line length angle
  if count < 36 then
    set line length to line length - 2
  if count > 36 then
    set line length to line length + 2
  change angle by 5
  change count by 1

define Line length angle
turn ↻ angle degrees
move length steps

If the count is less than 36, decrease the line length
If the count is greater than 36, increase the line length

47

Project: Recursive Spiral

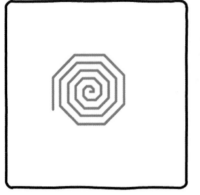

An interesting thing about functions is that they can call themselves. Whenever a function calls itself, it is called recursion. The only problem with this technique is that you need a way to stop the calling process or else the program will run forever!

If loops are helpful for stopping the program because you can tell the program to stop once a certain condition has been met. For example, you could initially call the loop with the variable "size" that has been initialized to 100. Each time the loop calls itself, the "size" decreases by 1. When the value of "size" reaches 0, the program will stop.

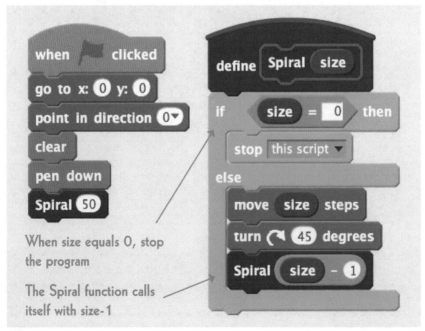

When size equals 0, stop the program

The Spiral function calls itself with size-1

Project: Dragon Curve

Programmers like recursion a lot because it lets them make really complicated drawings using relatively few lines of code. If you tried to draw the dragon curve above only by using functions and repeat loops, it would take you hours, and hundreds of lines of code, to complete.

Try experimenting with the code on the next page by calling the function with different inputs (for example call the function x with x 6 or x 13).

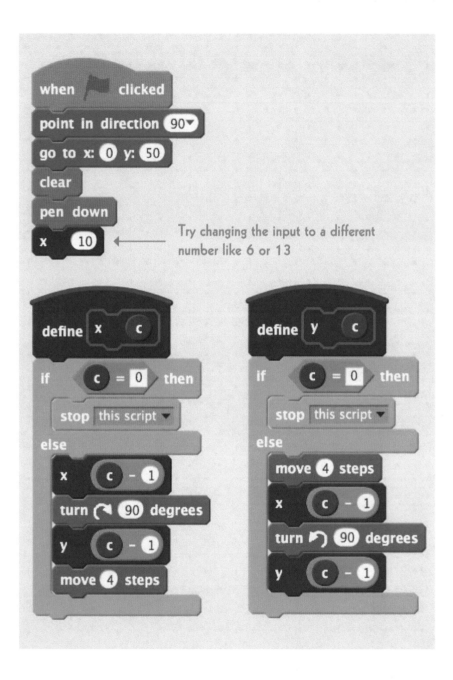

```
when [flag] clicked
point in direction (90▼)
go to x: (0) y: (50)
clear
pen down
x (10)
```

Try changing the input to a different number like 6 or 13

```
define x (c)
if ((c) = [0]) then
    stop [this script ▼]
else
    x ((c) - (1))
    turn ↻ (90) degrees
    y ((c) - (1))
    move (4) steps
```

```
define y (c)
if ((c) = [0]) then
    stop [this script ▼]
else
    move (4) steps
    x ((c) - (1))
    turn ↺ (90) degrees
    y ((c) - (1))
```

Project: Hilbert Curve

The labyrinth above is called the Hilbert curve. Like the dragon curve, it is really easy to draw with a recursive function.

After you copy the code on the next page into Scratch and run the program, try experimenting with altering the code. For instance, try changing the inputs for the lsec function call in the last line of code to lsec 5 5 or lsec 3 3.

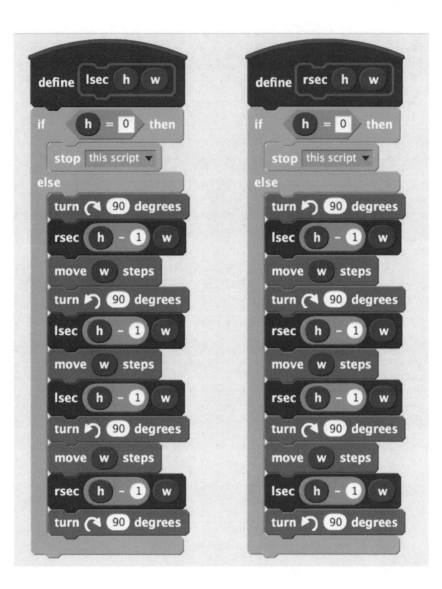

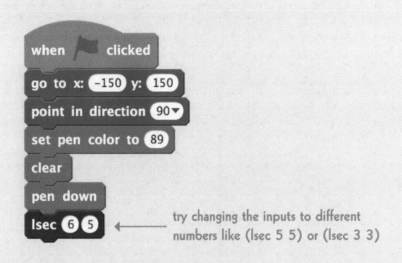

```
when 🚩 clicked
go to x: -150 y: 150
point in direction 90▾
set pen color to 89
clear
pen down
lsec 6 5
```

try changing the inputs to different
numbers like (lsec 5 5) or (lsec 3 3)

Ch 10: Practice Problems

1) Can you make a recursive spiral triangle?

2) Use the spiral triangle code from above to make a star. Experiment with different angles and lengths to create different types of stars.

Making Lists

11

So far we have only used Scratch to manipulate numbers and variables one value at a time, but we can also store and manipulate lists of things.

Lists Remember when you learned about variables? Variables are a way to store one thing in memory. Sometimes you need to store multiple things in memory but you don't want to do a lot of tedious typing. Lists let you store many values in a single structure.

Making Lists Making lists is like making a variable. Go to the Data Section and click the "*Make List*" button then enter the name of the list. You can then use the add block to add items to the list.

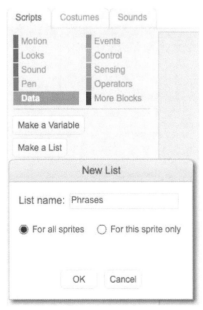

Project: Curses

This program is based on the work of Tom Dwyer and Margot Critchfield, who published a similar program in their book *BASIC and the Personal Computer* in 1979. It uses lists to create a computer generated poem.

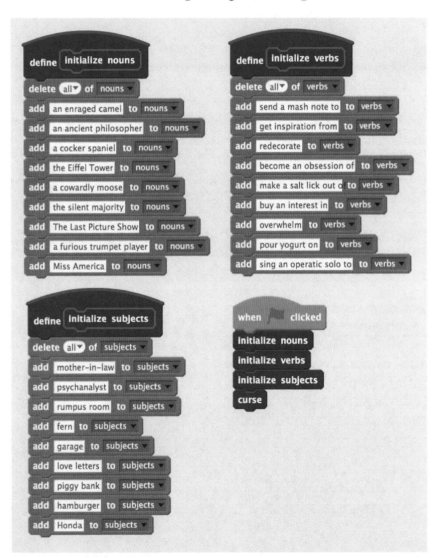

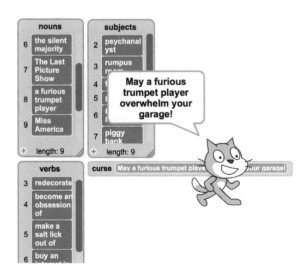

```
define curse

set curse ▾ to May

set curse ▾ to join curse  item random▾ of nouns ▾

set curse ▾ to join curse  [ ]

set curse ▾ to join curse  item random▾ of verbs ▾

set curse ▾ to join curse  your

set curse ▾ to join curse  item random▾ of subjects ▾

set curse ▾ to join curse  !

say curse
```

Change this program to suit your personality. Add more things to the lists. Take some things away. Change the pattern used to form the curse. Is the pattern for a blessing different from the pattern for a curse?

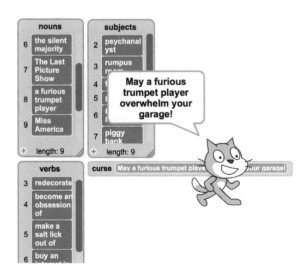

Ch 11: Practice Problems

1) Many computer programs have been developed that generate poetry or music. Some of them use a technique similar to the curses program. These programs often have large lists of words that are arranged according to some predefined patterns.

For example, you might draw from lists in a pattern like this:

Title
Adjective Noun
Verb Noun
Noun Preposition Noun Verb Noun
  Ending Phrase

How could you make your poem rhyme? How could you link the Title and Ending Phrase to give your poem a sense of order and completion?

2) Working in a group, modify your program so that it generates poetry instead of curses. Within your group, select your three favorite computer generated poems.

3) Try making a program that generates haikus. A haiku is a short Japanese poem that consists of 3 lines. The first and last lines of a Haiku have 5 syllables and the middle line has 7 syllables. The lines rarely rhyme.

4) Make a Dadaist poem in the style of Tristan Tzara:
    a. Take a newspaper.
    b. Choose an article as long as you are planning to make your poem.
    c. Make a list containing each of the words that make up this article.
    d. Make a poem by randomly choosing each word.

Remove the word from the list after it
is used.
e. The poem will be like you.

And here [is the computer] a writer, infinitely original
and endowed with a sensibility that is charming though
beyond the understanding of the vulgar.

~Tristan Tzara

Problem Solutions

2: First Program

1) There are many ways to draw a house. The code below shows one way to draw a house by first drawing the rectangle and then adding a triangle to the top of the image.

```
when [flag] clicked
go to x: 0 y: 0
point in direction 90▾
clear
pen down
move 100 steps
turn ↻ 90 degrees
move 100 steps
turn ↻ 90 degrees
move 100 steps
turn ↻ 90 degrees
move 100 steps
turn ↻ 90 degrees
turn ↺ 45 degrees
move 70 steps
turn ↻ 90 degrees
move 70 steps
```

2) A diamond can be drawn in many ways. The code below shows a simple way to draw a diamond.

```
when [flag] clicked
go to x: 0 y: 0
point in direction 90▾
clear
pen down
turn ↺ 45 degrees
move 100 steps
turn ↺ 90 degrees
move 100 steps
turn ↺ 90 degrees
move 100 steps
turn ↺ 90 degrees
move 100 steps
```

5: Repeat Command

1) There are many ways to draw different size circles. The code below shows one way to draw two different size circles. The first repeat code draws the smaller inner circle and the second repeat code draws the bigger outer circle.

```
when 🏴 clicked
go to x: 0 y: 0
point in direction 90▾
clear
pen down
repeat 360
    move 1 steps
    turn ↻ 1 degrees
point in direction 180▾
move 18 steps
point in direction 90▾
repeat 120
    move 2 steps
    turn ↻ 3 degrees
```

2) The easiest way to draw a hexagon is to draw 6 lines with an angle of 60 degrees between each line.

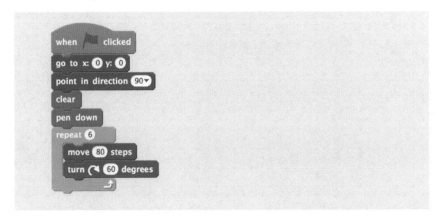

6: Nested Repeats

1) There are many ways to draw a shape consisting of hexagons. The code below describes one way to draw the shape.

```
repeat 8
    repeat 6
        move 80 steps
        turn ↻ 60 degrees
    turn ↻ 45 degrees
```

2) The code below describes one way to draw a shape made out of many circles.

```
repeat 15
    repeat 36
        move 10 steps
        turn ↻ 10 degrees
    turn ↻ 24 degrees
```

8: All About Variables

1) False. Since the computer thinks lower and upper case letters are different, 'myFirstVariable and 'MYFIRST-VARIABLE do not mean the same thing to the computer.

2) The final value of w is: **12**

3) The final value of w is: **16**

9: Awesome Functions

1) There are many ways to create a function that draws triangles. Below is one way to do it.

```
define triangle length
repeat 3
    move length steps
    turn ↻ 360 / 3 degrees
```

2) The code below shows you one way to draw a resize-able house.

```
define house length
go to x: 0 y: 0
point in direction 0▾
pen down
repeat 4
    move length steps
    turn ↻ 360 / 4 degrees
move length steps
turn ↻ 30 degrees
repeat 4
    move length steps
    turn ↻ 360 / 3 degrees
pen up
```

10: If Statements

1) There are many ways code a recursive triangle. Below is one way to do it.

```
define triangleSpiral x

if   x = 0   then
    stop this script ▼

move x steps
turn ↻ 360 / 3 degrees
triangleSpiral x - 10
```

2) To create the star in the picture provided, use this code:

```
when ⚑ clicked
go to x: 0 y: 50
point in direction 90▼
pen down
clear
repeat 8
    triangleSpiral 100
    turn ↻ 15 degrees
    move 100 steps
```

```
define triangleSpiral x

if   x = 0   then
    stop this script ▼

move x steps
turn ↻ 360 / 3 degrees
triangleSpiral x - 10
```

Useful Resources

Scratch Home Page
http://www.scratch.mit.edu

Snap! Home Page
http://snap.berkeley.edu

The Beauty and Joy of Computing
http://bjc.berkeley.edu/website/curriculum.html

Learn Scratch
http://learnscratch.org

Scratch for Budding Computer Scientists
http://cs.harvard.edu/malan/scratch/index.php

Made in the USA
Lexington, KY
17 August 2016